T0132169

Read My Mind...
See My Thoughts

THEODORA YELDELL MAYS

BALBOA.
PRESS
A DIVISION OF HAY HOUSE

Balboa Press books may be ordered through booksellers or by contacting:

Balboa Press
A Division of Hay House
1663 Liberty Drive
Bloomington, IN 47403
www.balboapress.com
1 (877) 407-4847

Because of the dynamic nature of the Internet, any web addresses or links contained in this book may have changed since publication and may no longer be valid. The views expressed in this work are solely those of the author and do not necessarily reflect the views of the publisher, and the publisher hereby disclaims any responsibility for them.

The author of this book does not dispense medical advice or prescribe the use of any technique as a form of treatment for physical, emotional, or medical problems without the advice of a physician, either directly or indirectly. The intent of the author is only to offer information of a general nature to help you in your quest for emotional and spiritual well-being. In the event you use any of the information in this book for yourself, which is your constitutional right, the author and the publisher assume no responsibility for your actions.

Any people depicted in stock imagery provided by Thinkstock are models, and such images are being used for illustrative purposes only.
Certain stock imagery © Thinkstock.

Print information available on the last page.

ISBN: 978-1-5043-9545-8 (sc)
ISBN: 978-1-5043-9546-5 (e)

Balboa Press rev. date: 05/01/2018

Contents

Acknowledgement Page

I was blessed to have been one of the 5,000 women present for a Woman's Conference in San Francisco, CA back in the 1990's in which Oprah Winfrey was a Keynote Speaker. One of the things she said that day that really stood out in my mind was the importance of surrounding yourself with "**DREAM PUSHERS**"and not DREAM KILLERS. Down through the years I have been blessed to have people in my life who have encouraged, supported and pushed me forward to succeed in my Writing endeavor. I therefore wish to give back by listing them in this Acknowledgement Page of this my first book publication.

SPECIAL HONORABLE MENTION TO SOME *EXTRA SPECIAL DREAM* PUSHERS!!!

Evelyn E. Yeldell Salisbury, NC

(My wonderful deceased mother) It was my desire to have had my mother to see my name in writing before she left this world. Unfortunately, I didn't move swiftly enough; but she was always encouraging, supportive and proud of me! She was my #1 Cheerleader!!!

Elder T.R. Yeldell

My deceased father of whom I was named after. He was always opened to listen to and participate in my various forms of artistic Writings and encouraged me to do my best.

Elder Clifford Mays

My Wonderful, Dear and Precious husband of 35 beautiful blessed years!
My friend, my lover, my greatest encourager, my supporter, listener, advisor, promoter, and my **ROCK!!!**

Roslyn L. Yeldell - Salisbury, NC

My oldest Sister who repeatedly push, encouraged & supported me to pursue my Writing until I did it!

Trina Brigham – San Francisco, CA

A Great Friend, Sister in the Lord, Mentor and the one who made me dig deep down within myself and bring out MORE that what was hidden inside me. (Read...... "What's Her Name?") Trina Brigham is an AMAZING WRITER herself and she still took the time to put me on the right road to acquiring this Book Publisher.

Diane Thompson – San Francisco, CA

A wonderful friend! One night I made the statement, *"One day I want to be a Writer"*....The power of her response **_made me_** take ownership of my Gift as she **proclaimed,.....** "St.T, You **ARE A WRITER**"!!!

Annie Caldwell – San Francisco, CA

My hero, advisor, counselor, my 88 year old Mentor who has been one of the most inspiring encouraging people in my life! She believed in me and has given me so much love & wisdom!

Elder Derrick White – San Francisco, CA

My former Pastor and a Musical Artist who has been very encouraging to me and has inspired me not to be afraid to be me and to express myself through the deep thoughts of my Writings.

My Other Special Dream Pushers

Vintricia Alexander – San Francisco, CA
Sherry Mings/Bevans – San Francisco, CA
Valerie Scott Martinsville, VA (Neice)
Wendy Harris-Hunter – Charlotte, NC
Katrina Grier – Charlotte, NC
Marcelle Herron – Miami Fla.
Andrea Y. Ward – Martinsville, VA (Sister)
Michaune Ogiale – Seattle, WA
Tina Davis – San Francisco, CA
Joseph Lewis – Charlotte, NC
Antonia Mixson – Salisbury, NC (Neice)
Kim Carter – San Francisco, CA
Esteen Williams – Los Angeles, CA
Deborah Gilliam-Salisbury, NC
Rosa Maxwell Green – Salisbury, NC
Robin Kelley – San Francisco, CA
Brenda Huff – Washington, DC
Lakisha Ward – Richmond, VA (Niece)
Jennifer C. Ward – Richmond, VA (Niece)
Thea Holmes – Seattle, WA (My Beautician)
Terry Holmes – Seattle, WA (My Photographer)
Patricia Cheadle – Seattle, WA
LaTonya Ausler – Seattle, WA

A Mother's Reward

By Theodora Mays

A mother gives birth in sorrow and bears pains of
labor that cause her to weep and mourn.
But her heart is filled with love & joy when she beholds
the face of the precious baby that she has born.

A mother patiently cares for and is constantly
awakened by her baby's cries during the evening,
late night and even at the crack of dawn.

A mother puts her child's needs first before hers; working to
support her family even when her body's tired and worn.

The responsibilities of a mother aren't easy and are
filled with many days of weathering the storm.

A mother deals with doctor visits, school
preparations, and religious and children events
and lots of other things nine yards long.

A mother instills good morals and values in her child from their
youth and teen years all the way until they're fully grown.

The reward a child can give a mother is to show
they were raised God-fearing, respectful of others,
life equipped and to be wise and strong.

Lord, I Thank You.

By Theodora Yeldell Mays

Lord, I thank you for the strong tall standing trees.
Thank you for the warm sunshine and for the cool pleasant breeze.
Thank you for the array of flowers you created so beautifully.
Thank you for the great waters of the oceans and the mighty seas.

Lord, I thank you for the blessing of a wonderful mother.
Thank you for my Dad, my sisters and my brother.
Thank you for food, clothing and for shelter from the weather.
Thank you for our relationship that's like none other.

Lord, I thank you for the lessons that this life teaches.
Thank you for your Holy Word that my Pastor preaches.
Thank you for all the needy people your mercy reaches.
Thank you for giving us your Precious Son Jesus.

Lord, I thank you for the moon the stars for the snow and for the rain.
Thank you for the good times as well as for the pain.
Thank you for so many blessings that I just can't explain.
I Thank you, Thank you, Thank you Lord for everything.

Loving through the suffering

By Theodora Yeldell Mays

When the Sons of God came up before His thrown, Satan came along with them.

God asked Satan, "What has he been doing and where all has he been?"

He told God, *"I've been seeking to devour souls on the earth walking up and down in it wandering."*

God asked Satan, "Have you considered my servant Job? He's perfect and upright and eschew sin."

"Yes", Satan replied: *"But because of your hedge, I can't get to him."*

God knew if he removed the hedge that the degree of Job's love and faith were strong enough to endure any amount of suffering.

So God removed the hedge from around Job and this is when the challenge of his love & faith began.

Soon Satan caused Job to lose all his possessions along with the sudden death of his seven grown children.

When all these trials & loss didn't shake his love and faith....Satan asked God for consent to touch his skin.

God granted permission for Satan to touch Job's flesh which meant his body would now feel Satan's hands on him.

Job sat down in sack cloths and ashes while scratching the boils that completely covered his face, head, body and limbs.

His acquaintances came to visit but instead of giving comfort, love and support; their words were judgmental, critical, and insulting him.

Job knew he had done no wrong nor was he guilty of committing any sin.

To sum things up, Job's Faith and Love endured the trails of losing his wealth and family destroyed by a great wind.

The next time you start to complain and get upset about trials facing you, remember Job's example of "Loving through the suffering."

3

What Does God See..... When He's Looking Down At You And Me??

By Theodora Yeldell Mays

What does God see when He's looking down at you and me?
Does He see us living as God-fearing, God-loving, obedient children of His? Or...
Does He see us breaking His commandments, hating one another and behaving like we're the Devil's kids?

Does He hear us speaking gentle, kind and loving words and feeling the care of one another? Or...
Does He hear us fussing, cussing, lying, back-biting and speaking harsh words to our sisters and our brother?

Does He see us living holy lives and keeping his commandments to prove to Him our love? Or...
Does He see us willfully committing sinful acts not caring that He's watching us from above?

Does God see us pressing our way to His House regularly to pray, to testify and to give Him praises? Or...
Does He see us sitting home idle while his House and our daily bread is being wasted?

Does He hear us complaining and grumbling about what we don't have and all the things that seem to be going wrong? Or...
Does God hear us being grateful for whatever we do have and see us using our challenges to make us strong?

What does God see when He's looking down at you and me??

I don't know about you…..but I want Him to see me as an outstanding example of Holiness and someone who loves Him with their whole body, mind and soul…..
And I want Him to see me as an obedient doer of His word with fervent and perfect Love for my fellowman that will never wax cold.

The Right or the Wrong you do when you're *YOUNG* can Benefit or Hamper you in years to come.

By Theodora Mays

It's important to make careful decisions when you're young
Because the results of your actions can affect you in years to come.
From a child we're taught to eat vegetables & fruits, like apples, bananas, oranges and plums....
Because eating only greasy, starchy and sugary foods can down the road lead to health problems.

It's important to make careful decisions when you're young
Because the results of your actions can affect you in years to come.
Parents send their children to school to learn so they can make something of themselves and not end up a bum.....
Which can happen when you refuse to learn from the teachers, the experiences of others and the older people's words of wisdom.

It's important to make careful decisions when you're young
Because the results of your actions can affect you in years to come.
Ignoring warnings against indulging in sexual activities, thinking you're grown and having your fun....
Could cause you months later you to hear the words, *"You **are** the **Father**"* or some dud's *"baby's mama"* raising a daughter or a son.

It's important to make careful decisions when you're young
Because the results of your actions can affect you in years to come.
Following after friends who indulge in smoking, drinking, cursing and cutting people with their tongue

Could leave you messed up, addicted, or behind bars for something stupid you've done.

It's important to make careful decisions when you're young
Because the results of your actions can affect you in years to come.
Tattooing your body with the name of that *"current person"* in your life or some colorful drawing you envisioned......
Can leave you **"SCARRED"** after the fad has faded and future generations wondering,
"What planet did *YOU come from??!*

It's important to make careful decisions when you're young
Because the results of your actions can affect you in years to come.
If you marry a guy just because he's good looking or a female just because she's a pretty woman
Could result in their ugly and disrespectful ways making life miserable for you and for your children.

The Right or the Wrong you do when you're young
can Benefit or Hamper you in years to come.
Eating right and taking care of yourself can have you in your 40's looking and feeling like you're 21.
Remembering your Creator in the days of your youth will bring great blessings and God will help you to overcome.

The Right or the Wrong you do when you're YOUNG
can Benefit or Hamper you in years to come.
Your peers may make laugh at you because you don't do what they do and run where they run.
But you'll have joy and peace inside from seeking first after God's righteousness and His Kingdom.
The Right or the Wrong you do when you're YOUNG
can Benefit or Hamper you in years to come.

The Time Of Our Lives

By Theodora Yeldell Mays

There are so many things we can do.....if we'd only take the Time to get them done.

There are so many dawns we can see awakening.....if we'd take the Time to watch the rising of the sun.

There are so many self-improvements we can make...... if we'd take the Time to begin with just one.......and the only Time we have is......
The Time of our Lives.

There are so many people who we can uplift.....If we'd take the Time to lend a hand.

There are so many issues in which we can cast our vote.....If we'd take the Time to express where we stand.

There is so much of this great world for us to see.....If we'd take the Time to travel this great land.......and the only Time we have is.......
The Time of our lives.

There are so many things for us to see......If we'd only take the Time to look.

There is so much important matter to be learned.....If we'd take the Time to read a book.

There are so many different meals to be prepared......If we'd only take the Time to cook.....and the only time we have is........*The Time of our lives.*

There is so much happiness we can give.....if we'd take the Time to do a good deed.

There is so much aid we can provide......If we'd take the Time to help those in need.

There are so many good works we can sow......If we'd take the Time to plant a seed......and the only time we have is.......**THE TIME OF OUR LIVES.**

What Will I Be Like; When I'm Grown??

By Theodora Mays

Before the break of dawn…..
So early in the morn…..
I feel a touch…..A tender kiss….
I hear a noise they call an alarm.

My warm blankets hurriedly pulled back…..
I feel gentle pat……I yawn and stretch my body…..
Then I curl up like a cat.

I'm lifted from out of my crib…..
Whining like any sleepy kid……
I'm quickly dressed……Fed so fast…..
Food *spills all over* my bib!

I'm hauled out in the street……
Then strapped into a bulky car seat…….
I feel knocks…..Jerks…..and bumps…..phew……
My little body already feels beat!

We're suddenly not moving no more……
A strange woman comes to the door……
I'm lifted up……. and handed out……
I CRY so **HARD** *my eyes become sore*!

I *finally* settle down………
Other babies all around…..
I feel all alone like a puppy….who's been dropped off…..
at a dog pound.

We crawl around like ants and worms......
While playing and spreading each other's germs.....
Then we're made to sleep.....eat and we're taught.....
*WHATEVER **SHE*** wants us to learn.

THEN I **FINALLY** hear a familiar knock.....
I get SO happy and *excited **I COULD POP!**.....*
I Kick..... Laugh.....Stare and *SQUEAL*.......
In walks my mother,...........about to drop!

She *struggles* to gather me and my stuff.....
The ride back home is *even* **MORE ROUGH!**......
I SCREAM & HOLLER for her ATTENTION.....
She doesn't realize my **CRY** is no *bluff.*

What will I be like when I'm grown?......
When my mother doesn't teach and raise me at home.....
The years I need to develop...... and be nurtured should be cherished.....
For God gave me to my parents.......just as a loan.

WHAT'S HER NAME?

By Theodora R. Mays

She carefully places bandages over her wounds.......trying to conceal the pain.
She puts a blindfold over her eyes to shut out the darkened times in her life.....
to keep her confused mind sane.

She **generates** an inward **surge** of *power and energy* that is transmitted into *laughs* and *smiles* to compensate........ the hurt and distain.
She tapes a gag across her mouth; so no one can *distinguish* the muffled words behind it that she *mumbles* to herself ....in shame.
There's a hole in her heart and a void in her arms from the loss of a loved one she only talks to God about ....when she's praying.
Her hands are tied with ropes of fear that bind her from doing the things that will bring her........ wealth and fame.

She carries a huge chip on her shoulders making her lack of progress being the fault of others and her *circumstances*........ the reason and the blame!

She's........*Sombody*!!!........She's..........
Everybody!!..........She's........*Anybody*!!!.....

CAN *YOU* give her a *name*???

While I'm Alive

By Theodora Mays

While I'm alive; I want to REALLY LIVE!
While I'm alive; I want to FREELY GIVE!
I want my deeds to express REAL LOVE!
I want my actions to please GOD UP ABOVE!

While I'm alive; I want to be a HELP!
While I'm Alive I want to handle any crisis I'm DEALT!
I want to think happy thoughts and speak words that are POSITIVE!
When I'm offered bad choices, I want to choose the OPPOSITE!

When I'm gone my name and my picture
will be a treasured MEMORY!
And the works of my life will be my LEGACY!
WHILE I'M ALIVE; I WANT TO REALLY LIVE!

DECEPTION.....DISTRACTION..... DISOBEDIENCE.... & DELIVERANCE

By Theodora Mays

DECEPTION initially began with the 1ˢᵗ woman God formed whom Adam
(her husband), named Eve.
The cunning serpent in the garden beguiled her with smooth enticing words that she listened to and believed.

DISTRACTION came the moment the serpent got her attention and she started looking at & desiring the fruit which she and Adam ate, not out of necessity, but out of curiosity and greed.

DISOBEDIENCE to God's instruction made Him upset, disappointed and
very sorely displeased.
God cursed the serpent and the two people He had formed and caused their sin to affect all humanity.

First came **DECEPTION**.....next **DISTRACTION** and then **DISOBEDENICE** which came thirdly.
Centuries later, God sent His Son Jesus to redeem man with His blood; this is how **DELIVERENCE** came to be.

Today in a world of so much **DECEPTION, DISTRACTION & DISOBEDIENCE** let's learn from man's early history.
Let's focus on obeying and praising God and thanking Jesus for our **DELIVERENCE** through His Blood which set us free.

Ms. Annie Caldwell

(who's Indian name is Annie Flagg)
Written by Theodora Mays about a very dear Sr. at church)

Annie Caldwell is an exceptional outstanding
Senior whose given name was Annie Flagg.
She dwells on positive, empowering thoughts about
herself that she repeats to herself, energizing her
faith, and it's not something she does to brag.

She has beautiful wrinkle free skin, a super sharp mind
but she becomes uncomfortable when she sits too long
ever since her "personal seat cushion" has began to sag.

Yet, because she's so resourceful, she remedies the problem
by carrying a large brown stuffed pillow packed
down inside of her big red cloth bag.

She's a pleasant, happy, free spirited little lady always
anxious to pull off her next big project even if it
has to be pushed, shoved, carried or dragged.

She learned at the San Francisco Conservatory of Music
and is knowledgeable in all types of singing plus she was
trained to sing classical music at a very early age.

She sounds SO BEAUTIFUL singing acapella; but when
you hear her musically accompanied by our talented Pastor,
Elder Derrick White, all you can say is just...

"DAGG!!!"

She loves to give in church; but when there's a delay
it's because she's looking for her checkbook, her
glasses or a pen, causing a little time lag.

She believes in getting what she wants....because
she wants it... and how many of it she wants....
and not worrying about what's on the price tag.

Ms. Annie, on this your special day and every day
we honor you for your love, your wisdom and the joy
you bring to our lives; and no matter what last name
has been added, you'll always be Annie Flagg.

It Makes Me Want To Cry

By Theodora Yeldell Mays

Lord, when I think about how good you've been to me…..
It makes me want to cry.

When I think about the horrible death your Son died to set me free…..
It makes me want to cry.

When I see how you're dishonored and people take your blessings so nonchalant and so ungratefully…It makes me want to cry.

When I think about how the disciples disowned & betrayed your Son so unfaithfully….It makes me want to cry.

When I think about times I disobeyed you over and over again…..
It makes me want to cry.

When I think about how grateful I am that you forgave me of my sins…
It makes me want to cry.

When I see how man doesn't acknowledge your creation and ALL the magnificent things you still do…It makes me want to cry.

Lord, when I'm praising your name and trying to express how very much

I DEEPLY LOVE YOU……I CRY!!

WHY WAIT FOR DEATH .....TO BRING OUR YOUR BEST?

By Theodora Yeldell Mays

Why not send a card or flowers to someone *now* rather than when they're down on their last sick bed???

Why wait to say, *"I'm sorry"*, to someone when they're lying across the altar .....cold, stiff and dead???

Why wait to express your love and respect for someone after they're gone *when* you could have expressed it when they were alive instead???

Why wait for Death to bring out your Best?

Why not take advantage of new opportunities *now* and stop letting fear of the unknown make you afraid???

Why not enjoy visiting family or friends *now* rather than when they're unable to enjoy you or incapable of understanding what's being said???

Why not give a person a call when they come across your mind before *you get a call* hearing the sad news that you'll dread???

Why wait for Death to bring out your Best?

Why not get your insurance matters in place now, rather than leaving grieving family members to be left in the red?

Why not walk into God's House *now* while you're able to come on your own and can get your daily bread???

Why wait to have to be *"rolled"* into God's House when you can neither eat the Word of God nor the Repass food that your family is fed????

WHY wait for Death to bring out your Best???

Black Brother!!....
Black Sister!!....
You Are A Testament Of
God's Magnificentness!

By
Theodora Mays

Black Brother and Black Sister, you are a
testament of God's Magnificentness
through the expression of your creativeness
which is an illumination of God's esteem Greatness
that is demonstrated when your ambitiousness
pushes through the thoughts in your mind
forcing it's wide openness
revealing your hidden gifts that explodes
God's extraordinariness of your being
Black Brother...Black Sister!!

Peace

BY Theodora Y. Mays

For Centuries, the world's been seeking for PEACE
And still has yet to find it.
It's more to obtaining **PEACE** from a war than merely saying,
"We Quit".

When gang members kill and races discriminate,
thinking they're better than the other.
They protest for **PEACE** from the war;
Yet they have hatred in their hearts for their brother.

PEACE is when every individual forgives, gets along with and has love
in his heart for his neighbor.
Yet **PEACE** will never fully come, until it's the will of our Creator.

God Has Feelings Too

By Theodora Yeldell Mays

How do you feel when you trust someone to pay you the money they owe you........**but they won't?**

How do you feel to constantly give food, clothing and shelter to someone and at least expect them to say, "Thank you"......
but they don't?

How do you feel when you constantly do nice things for someone who should gladly do the least little thing for you,........ **but they won't?**

How do you feel when you give a person the best of what you have and look for them to give you their best,......... **but they don't?**

How do you feel to always be there for someone and expect them to speak up and at least testify for you,........... **but they won't?**

How do you feel to uplift someone up when they're down and think they'd appreciate and remember you,................ **but they don't?**

How do you feel to be the answer to someone's prayers and then need them to answer your call,.......... **but they won't?**

The way we can be mistreated by people can leave us with feelings that are **hurtful, painful and real!**

Now **relate each of these questions** to the way

YOU treat God......

then ask yourself......*"How do I make GOD feel?"*

If Your Tears Could Talk....
What Would They Say?

BY Theodora Yeldell Mays

If your tears could talk, what would they say?
What outpour of pain and sadness would their words convey?
What heartfelt words of repentance would your tears pray?
How would they describe your grief & sorrow in an understandable way?

If your tears could talk, what would they say?
How would they express your hurt, your feelings, and your misery?
What words would describe the toll bad choices have caused you to pay?
How would they describe your grief and your sorrow in an understandable way?

And.....If Jesus' tears could talk, what would they say?
What words could describe the emotions he felt at Gethsemane?
What words would explain His Love by fulfilling his destiny?
How would they explain His pain and His suffering His shame and His agony?
If Jesus tears could talk.....what would they say?

Oh Summer Is A Fun Time!

By Theodora R. Mays
(My first poem written in the 3rd Grade)

Oh summer is a fun time…..
When everything is just fine!
There's no school to go to.
There's no homework to do.
There's just your playing friends and you!

Oh summer is a fun time….
When everything is just fine!
You can go to the playground and play.
You can go to the park and stay all day.
You can even go visit your Cousin May.

Oh summer is so much fun…..
When all the children like to jump and run!
The boys go to the woods and pick some plums
And the girls go buy some bubble gum.

There's A Blessing In The Storm

By Theodora Yeldell Mays

Today, someone, somewhere lost their home.
Somewhere, someone's loved one's gone.
If you experience this too…..
Just know God will see you through…..keep holding on.
There's a blessing in the storm.

Somewhere, someone's lost their job.
Someone, some where's having it hard.
If you experience this too…..
Just know God will see you through…..keep holding on.
There's a blessing in the storm.

Someone, somewhere has a child in trouble.
Somewhere someone's an unhappy couple.
If you experience this too…..
Just know God will see you through…..keep holding on.
There's a blessing in the storm.

Someone, somewhere got news they dreaded.
Someone, somewhere been falsely arrested.
If you experience this too…..
Just know God will see you through…..keep holding on.
There's a blessing in the storm.

Somewhere, someone's in desperate need of money.
Somewhere, someone's condition is just not funny.
If you experience this too…..
Just know God will see you through…..keep holding on.
There's a blessing in the storm.

Have People Lost Their Minds??

By Theodora Mays

Remember when ladies dressed respectfully when going to a place of worship and wouldn't think of wearing pants or torn jeans as if they were going someplace leisure or going down to the mall?.......

Remember when people reverenced Sundays as the Lord's Day and wouldn't dare go to a stadium and sit up watching any sport teams play ball?.......

Remember when people would have rebelled if the Government disobeyed God's orders and allowed same-sex marriages to be sanctioned and be accepted into our Country's law?...... Have people lost their minds?

Remember when the pursuit of happiness was everyone having equal rights to have food, to have clothing and to have housing, whether they were male or female, black or white, good or bad, rich or poor?.....

Remember when parents taught their children to obey and respect their teachers and would never have dared went to their child's school to have an open parent/teacher quarrel?.....

Remember when the airlines let the public fly their luggage free and did not charge them huge unfair amounts making travelers upset, mad and sore?......

Have people lost their minds?

Remember when people had a dispute they would fight it out in the streets using words, then maybe hands and fists but not guns and knives when they had a brawl?......

Remember when people were obsessed with having clear and unblemished skin and would never have considered walking around with a tattooed body looking like a human mural?....

Remember when people used their brains to remember phone numbers instead of using their finger to hit the contact feature on their cell phone to give someone a call?.....Have people lost their minds?

Remember when people could contact a business and immediately get a human & not a recording for you to push so many numbers until you'd be ready to climb a wall?.....

"Have people lost their minds?"….. (This last question could make even the sanest person with lots of patience almost loose it all!)

If you only KNEW What you *REALLY* NEED'A DO........ While you're alive

By Theodora Mays

I need'da go back to school.
Rent's due again.
I need'da loose some weight.
My car needs fix'ng.

Did I kiss my husband bye?
I need'da get my hair done.
My phone bill's due on Friday!
I should call my Mom.

I need'da put some clothes in the cleaners.
I need'da go to the dentist.
I need'da make more money.
I'll be glad when this day is finished.

I need'da get some clothes out of the cleaners.
What do I feel like eating tonight?
I need'da make more money.
I'll just stop somewhere and grab a bite.

*SUDDENLY..........*BOOOOOOOOMMMMMMM!!!!!
**BAAAANNNGGGGGGGGG!!!!!! LAVA OF FIRE!!!! SCREAMS
OF HORROR!!!**

BUILDING CALLASPES!!!!!

I DIE. EVERYTHING STOPS.

Don't Wait Too Late To Congradulate

By Theodora Yeldell Mays

When you see someone perform a commendable deed choosing the
right and not the wrong.
When you hear someone beautifully sing a soul-stirring song.
Don't let Satan fill your heart with jealousy and hate.
Don't wait too late to congratulate.

When you hear a minister deliver a message
that hits straight to your soul.
When you see someone now prospering and
able to wear diamonds and gold.
Don't let Satan fill your heart with jealousy and hate.
Don't wait too late to congratulate.

When someone cooks a dish that deliciously satisfies your taste.
When you see someone looking neat and trim or
see someone progressing in losing weight.
Don't let Satan fill your heart with jealousy and hate.
Don't wait too late to congratulate.

When someone performs a function so much
better than you ever could have done.
When someone achieves a goal or wins a prize
that you was hoping to have won.
Don't let Satan fill your heart with jealousy and hate.
Don't wait too late to congratulate.

"Esteem one another more than yourself",
is what the bible teaches us to do.

It also says for us to, "Do unto others as you
would have them do unto you."
We ALL have great qualities, talents and attributes that we know we
possess within ourselves;
But how much better would it feel to hear it
validated by the mouth of someone else??

How would you feel to hear the news that....That person
who you would *never even compliment*........is now dead.
Then you'll feel guilt & remorse because of the uplifting words you
never went to them & said.
So don't let Satan fill your heart with jealousy and hate.
Don't wait too late to congratulate.

Man owns nothing in this world But sells everything on earth.

By Theodora Mays

God freely supplied the earth with land, man sells it for his own profit.
God freely supplied the earth with water, man sells it for his own gain.
God freely supplied the earth with scenic beauty, man sells it for his own profit.
God freely supplied the earth with everything we see now and the things that were here first.
Man owns nothing in this world, but sells everything on earth.

God freely supplied the earth with flowers, man sells them for his own profit.
God freely supplied the earth with trees, man sells them for his own gain.
God freely supplied the earth with fruits and vegetables, man sells them for his own profit.
God is the cause of every living creature's existence from its birth.
Man owns nothing in this world, but sells everything on earth.

God freely supplied the earth with animals, man sells them for his own profit.
God freely supplied the earth with fish and seafood, man sells them for his own gain.
God freely supplied the earth with herbs and minerals, man sells them for his own profit.
God gave the ground man kills his fellowman for declaring it to be his turf.
Man owns nothing in the world, but sells everything on earth.

God sends down the necessities for man's spirit as blessing that He keeps stored up in heaven.
If they were within man's reach down here on earth, he'd sell them for a million seven.
Man accumulates earthly possessions like they're his to forever hold.
What profithed a man to gain this whole world and lose his soul?

Man owns nothing in this world, but sells everything on earth.

There's A Blessing In The Storm

By Theodora R. Mays

Today, someone, somewhere lost their home.
Somewhere, someone's loved one's gone.
If you experience this too…..
Just know God will see you through…..keep holding on.
There's a blessing in the storm.

Somewhere, someone's lost their job.
Someone, some where's having it hard.
If you experience this too…..
Just know God will see you through…..keep holding on.
There's a blessing in the storm.

Someone, somewhere has a child in trouble.
Somewhere someone's an unhappy couple.
If you experience this too…..
Just know God will see you through…..keep holding on.
There's a blessing in the storm.

Someone, somewhere got news they dreaded.
Someone, somewhere been falsely arrested.
If you experience this too…..
Just know God will see you through…..keep holding on.
There's a blessing in the storm.

Push Yourself Out Of Your Comfort Zone

By Theodora Yeldell Mays

The feeling of comfort and security started for
all of us before we were even born.
It began when we were snuggled in our mother's
womb; all comfy, protected and warm.
This feeling of *"peace and tranquility"* was all we knew
(for most folks), for about 9 months long.
But then there came a time we had to leave our familiar
space as our mother pushed us out of our comfort zone.
She pushed us out into a great big wide world
which would now become our new home.
Our senses were now exposed to sight, sound, hugs and
kisses and the relaxing music of her voice in a song.
We were pushed out also into a world full of commotion, hatred,
fussing, fighting.... and into a life that is trouble prone.
We'd experience heartaches, diseases, sicknesses, aches and
pains in our body in our muscles and in our bones.
We'd be exposed to eating good foods, having great friends, and
experience the awesome feeling God's presence when we're all alone.
We'd grow from the stages of developing as an infant, a
child, a teenager then finally becoming fully grown.
The new opportunities for us to fulfill in our lives are as limitless
as the galaxy is for our minds to expand and to roam.
There's a whole wide world of endless possibilities
that can materialize into rewarding realities when we
by faith now push our own selves out of our
Comfort Zone.

Got Strength?

By Theodora Yeldell Mays

The pain seems so unbearable.
Your mind, soul and body are exhausted and entangled with fear.
You just want this nightmare to be over with....
Including the smirks, rude comments and the eye piercing stare.

You feel like your very health is failing you.
You're so overwhelmed you breathe deeply grasping for air.
You don't want people to know your secrets
You make a conscious effort to keep smiling;
being careful not to show a tear.

It seems like everyone else is happy and prospering.
Which makes your situation seem to be "just not fair!"
When you felt like you exhausted all your help and resources....
Little did you know that God was watching;
even when you couldn't feel His care.

You didn't realize it was during your hardest times.....
God was still blessing you and had His
defending Angeles looming near.
He had to show you that He gave you what you asked Him for
When you said,.... "Lord, Give me Strength",.... in your prayer.

He knew how much you could take by the
amount of strength He put inside you...
But without a situation to use it; you wouldn't
even know your strength was there.
He wanted to see if you'd LOVE and
PRAISE Him unconditionally

Even when suffering through things that you
wouldn't want an enemy to share.

What you're going through now….. may
feel too HEAVY for you to carry.
But to put more on you than you can
handle…. God wouldn't dare!
The flesh of Job and Jesus became weak when
their strength was stretched to it's limit;
but the extreme extent of their pain & suffering;
would make anyone want to veer.

But God made them VICTORIOUS & PERFECT
EXAMPLES so that we all would be made aware…..
That when Loving Him & Trusting Him no
matter what the circumstances….
The EXTRAORDINARY REWARD of His
AWESOME BLESSINGS…..
won't be worthy to even compare.

Author Unknown

By Theodora Mays

Ever wondered.... what could the name of the person
who signs, *Author Unknown, possibly be?*

Could their name be Evelyn.....Diane.....
Crystal or Roslyn.....Clifford or Margery?

God gave that person the knowledge to express their
thoughts through a style of writing called Poetry.

God gave that person the wisdom to write words that are
passed down from generations touching minds perpetually.

God gave that person compassion to write words of comfort
for grieving loved ones in a church or a mortuary.

God gave that person the inspiration to write words
that become a song when adding a melody.

God gave that person the insight to describe the mystery
of his magnificent creation so precise and eloquently.

The next time you read a poem signed, Author
Unknown, and you wonder....
*"What could the **name** of that person **possibly be??"**

Just think....maybe that person ***realizes*** that their *"**GIFT**"* comes
from **God** and feel that signing ***His name*** would be forgery.

Why??

By Theodora Yeldell Mays

Why won't the Government stop the airlines from ripping off the traveling public from charging fees for luggage when there's no longer a fuel crisis??

Why do people disregard, disobey and disrespect God and only acknowledge Him when they're faced with troubles, disasters, fatal acts of racism or Isis?

Why does the FDA make struggling food businesses shut down on technical issues; yet allow big manufacturing companies to put harmful chemicals in our drinks & in our food??

Why don't Gays, Lesbians, and Transgenders realize that the government only endorses their equal rights, same sex marriages & AIDS to control the birthrate, so the population won't bloom??

Why do the Landlords make rents so high that people have to sleep outdoors, in cars & on the streets, while furry haired animals are indoors in a warm comfortable bed??

Why do people degrade a person and give them a hard way to go while they're alive but stop traffic to show their respect for a person when they're in a casket dead?

WHY??

Don't Die With Your Purpose Buried Inside

By Theodora Yeldell Mays

The reason thoughts, ideas and visions come to your mind
Is to show you what your purpose is
Before it's the end of your time.

No one else can do what you were created to do and to be.
But one thing you can know for sure
You were created with Greatness within thee.

You may have to climb up mountains of obstacles,
Float thru streams of problems
Swim over rivers of doubters
Step over rocks of disappointments
Face years of fears
But do whatever it takes
Despite the hardships and headaches
To serve using your God given talents
But above all fear God and keep his commandments.

From Pain To Power

BY Theodora R. Mays

This is a true story about a little girl from a small
town called Kosciusko Mississippi
She was raised in a home where she experienced
hardships and lived in poverty.
She even suffered a horrible abuse by a member of her own family.

At an early age, the churchwomen marveled at
her poise and her "speaking ability";
never imagining this profound trait would one
day make her a famous popular celebrity.
When her grandmother once declared, "Gal, you'll
have to wring out clothes like this someday".

>>>>>that was the key that unleashed her dreams and
determination as she proclaimed to herself,
"that'll never be me."
Growing up she made mistakes and received
scars from her "*falling in love' injuries*".
She once even had a cheating boyfriend to ask,
"Do you believe your *lying eyes or ME*?

Her life challenges have given her the insight
to open discussions of "people issues"
that were once thought of shamefully.

Through her **powerful struggle**, instead of her *struggling for power*
she's been blessed with a platform she used to make a
"positive" impact on humanity.
Because of her "light bulb moments", her unique
down to earth style and her genuine
expressions of love, her forum maintained its longevity.
Through mastering her own pains and challenges,......
countless hearts, minds and lives
have been touched, enlightened, shaped and
made happier, by the living and giving of

Oprah G. Winfrey.

I'm Too Blessed To Be Stressed

BY Theodora Yeldell Mays

"I'M TOO BLESSED TO BE STRESSED",
is a phrase that is a fact of life.......
and much more than just a rhyme.
Just stop right now....... Get pen and paper to jot down some things
that should easily come to your mind.
Now, speak these words out **LOUDLY** to yourself,....
"I'M TOO BLESSED TO BE STRESSED",
about 10 or 15 times.

As you start thinking about and writing out
your seen and unseen blessings....
you'll be amazed at all the unnoticed benefits you'll find.

Your list may show things like.... "I'm blessed that I'm able to
think, speak, hear, walk, talk, and I even have the ability to drive."
You may have written, "I'm blessed that I live in a country of
religious freedom, where there's plenty of food, clean water, houses,
shelters, schools, I got a job or I get money of some kind.

Your list may include the blessing of family, friends,
health, hands and feet and that you're able to sleep, eat
and that you thank God that you're not blind".

You may have jotted down that you're blessed that it wasn't you (or
anyone you knew) in that terrible accident; nor were you that person
brutally killed leaving grieving and upset family members behind.
Did you remember to list the occasions when you
should have gotten a ticket; but didn't and the incidents
when you were spared from paying a heavy fine?

Most of these blessings I listed here were given to you
freely from God and never costs you a dime.

If you really put your heart in doing this exercise; you'd be so full of
gratitude that by now, you should practically be feeling like crying.
If you can't list any blessings on your sheet; just get up.......go
look at that person in the mirror and say,...... "You're lying"!
Please keep your list with you to refer to especially on days
when things aren't going your way and you start getting
upset and begin to complain and start to whine.
The moral of this poem is....... If you keep the Attitude of Gratitude
& focus on your blessings ; you'll feel like you're gliding down
easy street even when you're struggling on an uphill climb.

"YOU'RE TOO BLESSED TO BE STRESSED".

Printed in the United States
By Bookmasters